P9-CRZ-826

FIRST AMERICANS

The Wampanoag

PAMELA DELL

Marshall Cavendish
Benchmark
New York

ACKNOWLEDGMENTS

Series consultant: Raymond Bial

Marshall Cavendish Benchmark
99 White Plains Road
Tarrytown, New York 10591-5502
www.marshallcavendish.us

Text, maps, and illustrations copyright © 2009 by Marshall Cavendish Corporation
Map on page 8 by XNR Productions, Inc. Map on page 15 by Rodica Prato
Craft illustrations by Chris Santoro

Text, maps, and illustrations copyright © 2009 by Marshall Cavendish Corporation

Library of Congress Cataloging-in-Publication Data
Dell, Pamela.
The Wampanoag / by Pamela Dell.
p. cm. — (First Americans)
Summary: "Provides comprehensive information on the background, lifestyle,
beliefs, and present-day lives of the Wampanoag people"—Provided by publisher.
Includes bibliographical references and index.
ISBN 978-0-7614-3024-7
1. Wampanoag Indians—History—Juvenile literature.   2. Wampanoag
Indians—Social life and customs—Juvenile literature.   I. Title.
E99.W2D48 2007
974.4004'97348—dc22
2007035867

Front cover: Wampanoag sisters and brother celebrate their heritage at a traditional festival.
Title page: Wampum beads, collected in a shell, were used as money and also in Wampanoag ceremonies.
Photo research by: Connie Gardner
Cover Photo by Marilyn "Angel" Wynn/NativeStock.com
The photographs in this book are used by permission and through the courtesy of: *NativeStock.com*: Marilyn "Angel" Wynn: 1, 4, 18, 20, 21, 24, 26, 27, 30, 33, 34, 35; *NorthWind Picture Archive:* 6, 7, 12, 13, 16, 17, 29; *Getty Images:* Hulton Archive, 11; *Gibson Stock Photography:* 25; *CORBIS:* 32, 36; *AP Photo:* Vincent De Witt, 38; Chitose Suzuki, 41.

Editor: Deborah Grahame
Publisher: Michelle Bisson
Art Director: Anahid Hamparian
Series Designer: Symon Chow

Printed in Malaysia
1 3 5 6 4 2

CONTENTS

1 · PEOPLE OF THE EARLY LIGHT

For at least ten thousand years before Europeans ever set foot on the eastern shores of North America, native peoples had been living there. Several different Indian nations populated the area that today is New England. One of these was the Wampanoag (Wam-puh-No-ug). Their name came from an Abenaki Indian word meaning "eastern people" or "people of the early light"—because the sun rises in the east.

As many as 30,000 Wampanoag lived throughout southeastern Massachusetts, the islands off the Massachusetts coast, and in present-day eastern Rhode Island. They lived by farming, fishing, and hunting.

Gradually, though, European explorers began to discover the "New World." They came looking for riches and adven-

The sun rises over eastern Cape Cod, home to the Wampanoag—the people of the early light.

Thousands of Wampanoag and other Native Americans suffered and died from deadly diseases brought by Europeans, as this hand-colored woodcut shows.

ture. But they brought deadly European diseases with them. This was a disaster for the native peoples. Not able to fight off these new diseases, thousands died. Entire villages were left with no one alive.

In November 1620 an English ship called the *Mayflower* sailed into waters off the coast of what today is Massachusetts.

The pilgrims' voyage aboard the *Mayflower* was long and difficult. A few died along the way, but most survived. One baby was even born during the voyage.

By then about three-quarters of the Wampanoag people had been wiped out. The *Mayflower* carried 102 European passengers. Most of them were pilgrims, people looking for religious freedom.

The pilgrims set to work building a small settlement on the Massachusetts coast. To them the land appeared to be

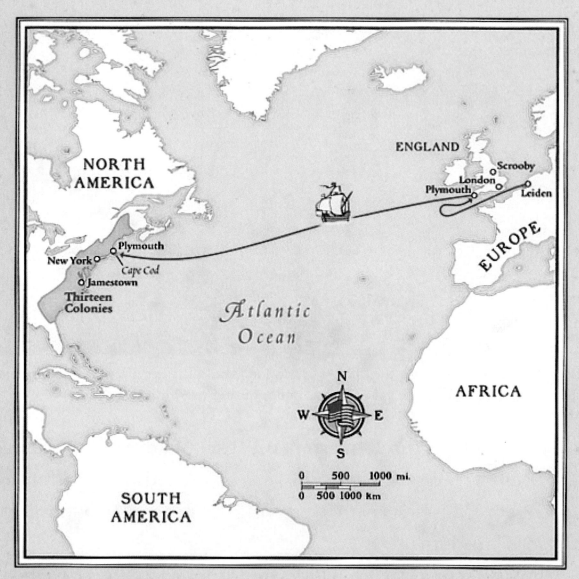

Many pilgrims started their journey to North America from Leiden in the Netherlands, as this map shows. They boarded the *Mayflower* in Plymouth, England, along with other travelers.

deserted. Nothing seemed to be left but the wild woods, empty fields where crops had once grown, and, here and there, scattered bones. The pilgrims were not aware that their settlement, which they called Plymouth Colony, stood where the Wampanoag village of Patuxet had once been.

Nearly unseen, the remaining Wampanoag stayed on their ancient homelands. They did not trust the Europeans, and wanted to avoid them. But as those early European colonists struggled to survive their first New England winter, the Wampanoag took pity on them. The Indians taught the colonists to fish and plant crops. Massasoit, the powerful grand **sachem**, met with the colonists in the early spring. Massasoit and the Plymouth colonists made a peace treaty. They promised to protect each other from neighboring enemies.

With the help of their Wampanoag neighbors, the pilgrims made it through the winter. In the fall of 1621 they celebrated their harvest with a thanksgiving feast.

Squanto

Only half the pilgrims made it through the winter of 1620–1621. Those who survived owed their lives to the Wampanoag as a group, but especially to one Wampanoag in particular. That man, named Tisquantum, or Squanto, walked into Plymouth Colony in March 1621 and began to speak English—a big surprise to the pilgrims. Because Squanto could communicate with them, he was able to teach the newcomers the Wampanoag methods of planting crops and fishing. Without this knowledge the pilgrims' "first Thanksgiving" would never have happened. Equally important, with Squanto acting as interpreter, Massasoit befriended the colonists.

Squanto, a Patuxet Wampanoag, had learned English through a series of encounters with the Europeans—not all of them good. More than once before meeting the pilgrims, Squanto had been kidnapped by visitors to the New World. In 1614 an Englishman named Thomas Hunt **lured** him onto a ship that was sailing for Spain. Hunt intended to make Squanto a slave, but once in Europe, Squanto escaped and eventually made his way to England. In 1619 he finally managed to return home— but by then his home had disappeared. Disease had **ravaged** his people, and the village of Patuxet was gone.

Two years later Squanto met the Plymouth colonists. This spelled the beginning of the end for the Wampanoag culture.

The Plymouth Colony pilgrims could not have survived
without Squanto's help.

As leader of the Wampanoag, Massasoit signed a peace treaty with the Plymouth colonists.

Massasoit attended the feast with ninety other Wampanoag. This celebration is known in the United States today as the first Thanksgiving.

The peace treaty between the Plymouth colonists and the Wampanoag lasted until Massasoit's death forty years later, in

1661. When Massasoit died his eldest son, Wamsutta, became grand sachem. Wamsutta died shortly after becoming sachem. Many suspected that the colonists had poisoned him during a visit he made to their settlement. This could not be proven. With Wamsutta gone, however, his younger brother, Metacomet, or Metacom, became the Wampanoag chief.

In Massasoit's years as leader, problems with the colonists had been growing. Thousands of newly arrived English settlers wanted more and more land. They tried to get Wampanoag lands by any means possible. Unlike the gentler early pilgrims, these later settlers did not

Wampanoag grand sachem Metacom, also known as King Philip by the English

respect the Wampanoag way of life. They let their animals run free all over Indian hunting grounds and farmlands. This damaged the Wampanoag food supply.

Metacom, known to the English as King Philip, was a tall, powerful, twenty-two-year-old warrior. He resented the colonists' damage to his people's lands and their efforts to take control of everything. He vowed to put a stop to it.

In June 1675 conflict broke out between the colonists and the Wampanoag. This was the beginning of what is known today as King Philip's War. Over several months Philip's warriors won many battles. But by the following spring the war was turning in the colonists' favor. Throughout the summer of 1676 they hunted down their Native American enemies. They burned villages to the ground and sold **captives** into slavery in the South.

On August 1, 1676, Philip's wife and nine-year-old son were captured. Then, in the early morning of August 12, 1676, colonists surrounded Philip's hideout. In a surprise attack they shot and killed him. The colonists cut off Philip's

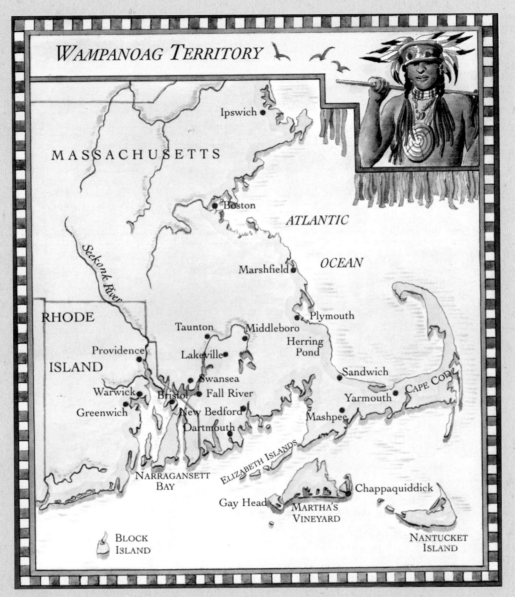

Wampanoag Territory

Ipswich

MASSACHUSETTS

Boston

ATLANTIC

OCEAN

Marshfield

Plymouth

Taunton   Middleboro

Herring
Pond

Providence   Lakeville

RHODE

Swansea

ISLAND

Warwick   Bristol   Fall River

Sandwich

Greenwich   New Bedford

Yarmouth   CAPE COD

Dartmouth

Mashpee

ELIZABETH ISLANDS

Chappaquiddick

NARRAGANSETT
BAY

Gay Head

MARTHA'S
VINEYARD

BLOCK
ISLAND

NANTUCKET
ISLAND

Seekonk River

This map shows Wampanoag territory as it was when the first European
colonists arrived in the early 1600s.

Fighting between the colonists and the Wampanoag was fierce during King Philip's War. This hand-colored woodcut shows the burning of Brookfield, Massachusetts, in 1675.

head. They carried their terrible trophy home to Plymouth and stuck it on a pole at the town gate. There it sat for the next twenty-five years.

By the end of King Philip's War in 1676, little was left of the Wampanoag culture. Unlike Native Americans in other

King Philip was shot to death in August of 1676, while he lay sleeping.

parts of colonial America, the Wampanoag were never forced off their native lands and relocated as a group by U.S. government orders. But many who had escaped death or slavery fled north or west to join other Indian nations.

Only about four hundred native people remained in the Massachusetts area, and they were nearly powerless. Most of them gave in and adopted Christianity and European customs. Today the descendents of those people still live on the land that King Philip once fought so hard to protect and save.

2 · THE WAMPANOAG WAY OF LIFE

The Wampanoag lived in harmony with the natural world around them. Their lives followed the cycle of the seasons. They hunted, farmed, and fished in the plentiful waters around them. In the spring and summer they lived near the ocean and tended their fields. When fall came they broke down their summer camps and moved to winter villages farther inland. They traveled on foot following trails through the forest, or by river in **dugouts**.

The Wampanoag's main crops were squash, beans, and corn, or maize. Known as the "three sisters," these crops were planted together instead of separately. They provided a balanced, nutritious diet. Women gathered nuts, seeds, and wild fruits and vegetables. Maple trees gave the Wampanoag

The woods and coastal waters held so much food that they were like supermarkets for the Wampanoag.

syrup. Men fished the ocean and fresh waters for herring, eel, cod, clams, mussels, and other shellfish. Many foods were dried and stored in underground containers, to be eaten later.

Quahogs, thick-shelled clams, were a special treat, but they were not just for eating. Quahog shells were threaded tightly together and called **wampum**. Wampum was used in religious ceremonies, as jewelry, and as money to trade for other goods.

After carving their canoes, or dugouts, from large logs, the Wampanoag soaked them in the river to make them watertight.

This is an inside look at a Wampanoag home, empty except for a sleeping platform.

In their summer camps the Wampanoag lived in small, round homes called *wetus*. These were single-family homes framed from the trunks of saplings, or young trees. The saplings were bent into a curved position and tied together. Then they were covered with mats woven of cattails and other materials.

Wampum

Modern-day people sometimes carry their cash in a money belt. The Wampanoag used wampum in much the same way. Wampum beads made from quahog shells were strung together. Often several single strands were woven to each other to fashion wide, beautiful belts and other decorative apparel. White wampum was plentiful, but the purple shells were harder to find. Deep purple beads were the most prized and valuable of all.

Since quahogs are not so easy for most people to come by, here's a fun way to create a little homemade wampum.

You will need:

- Pasta pieces—Small types of dry pasta, such as elbow macaroni, work best.
- Red food coloring and blue food coloring
- Rubbing alcohol*
- Thick colorful yarn or string

Before you begin, cover your workspace with paper towels, newspaper, or other inexpensive paper. Don't cook the pasta! Divide the uncooked pieces in half. Fill a bowl with enough rubbing alcohol to cover the pasta—but don't put the pasta in it yet. Add an equal number of drops of red and blue food coloring to the alcohol to get a good, deep purple color. Stir to blend the color.

Now carefully add half of the pasta to the bowl. Leave the pasta in the liquid just long enough for it to absorb the dye and reach the shade of purple you like. Then scoop it out with a slotted spoon and leave it to dry thoroughly. The noncolored half of the pasta will represent the white quahogs.

Cut one or more long pieces of yarn. Wrap tape around one end of the yarn to make it easy to thread the yarn through the pasta. Tie a big, tight knot at the other end of the yarn so the pasta won't slip off. String as many strands as you like. If you make multiple strands, try tying them together at certain points with small, strong bits of yarn or string, to make a wider piece. By experimenting with the placement of the "white beads" and pieces colored in various shades of purple, you might be able to come up with a very interesting design!

*Water can be substituted for alcohol, but the pasta shouldn't be left long in the water or it will become soft and sticky.

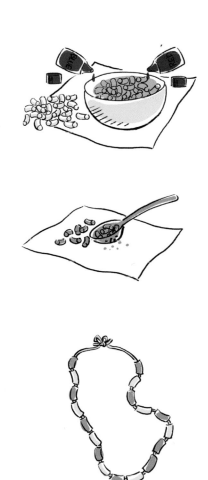

Wampanoag Corn Cakes

Try making a food that was a staple in the Wampanoag diet. You'll get about twenty corn cakes from this recipe, depending on how big you make them. Get a grownup to help you cook your corn cakes.

You will need:

- 1 cup of milk
- 1 cup of cornmeal
- 1 large egg
- 1 teaspoon of salt
- 1 teaspoon of sugar
- butter or vegetable spray

Bean cakes are another delicious variation of corn cakes.

Mix the egg and milk together. Then add the salt, sugar, and cornmeal. Stir into a thin batter. Spray a frying pan with vegetable spray or coat it with a thin layer of butter and heat it. When the pan is good and hot, drop spoonfuls of batter onto it, like you would do to make pancakes. When the edges begin to dry and bubbles appear, flip the corn cakes over and cook them on the other side. When they are firm and slightly golden colored, put them on a plate. Eat them plain or pour maple syrup over them, as the Wampanoag did. You can also eat them with butter, jam, or jelly.

The outside of well-made Wampanoag dwellings: on the left, a single-family wetu, and on the right, a house for two or more families

In the winter camps several families shared a "longhouse," or *nushwetu*. This dwelling was similar to the wetu, but shaped something like a long loaf of bread. The nushwetu was often covered in long strips of tree bark as well as matting.

In the woods men hunted black bear, deer, wild turkey,

A Wampanoag woman in a warm winter robe made of deerskin and fur, and decorated with paint

geese, and ducks. They trapped beaver, squirrels, raccoons, and rabbit. Some of the meat was smoked and dried and saved for winter, when live game was less available.

Animals provided tools and clothing as well as food. Summer dress was light, but the Wampanoag wore the furs of timber wolves, harbor seals, black bears, red foxes, and other mammals in winter. Many wore a garment called a **mantle**.

Most other clothing was made from deerskin. Elk and moose were rare, but were sometimes used, too. Wampanoag women scraped the hair off the skins and then "tanned" them—a process that made the skin soft and long-lasting. Women wore knee-length deerskin skirts, and men and women both wore deerskin leggings and shoes called **moccasins**.

The Wampanoag also made jewelry from shells, feathers, claws, beads, leather, and carved bone. Big, beautiful belts were made of wampum. Men and women both wore embroidered headbands. Feathers were added according to one's role in the tribe or achievements in battle.

Wampanoag women usually wore their hair in a long, single braid. Sometimes they added porcupine quills or other decorations. Older male tribal

A Wampanoag man in traditional dress, which was made from fur, animal skins, and cloth

members often wore a "Mohawk" style—their heads were shaved except for a strip of hair worn stiffly upright down the center of the skull. Boys began growing their hair long at about the age of sixteen, when they were considered old enough to be warriors.

Sports and games were important parts of tribal life. The Wampanoag enjoyed dice, tug-of-war games, and other kinds of contests. They competed in wrestling, swimming, **marksmanship**, and weight-lifting matches. Stickball, something like modern-day lacrosse, was a rough sport and fights sometimes broke out.

The grand sachem was in charge of overseeing all the villages and other sachems. But each community had its own sachem. The position of sachem was passed down through a family, and women as well as men served in this position of leadership. The sachems enjoyed some higher status and wealth, but they did not have many special privileges. Their role was mainly to give wise and trusted advice.

Other important roles in the tribe included the war chief and the **pnieses**, who were also leaders in battle. Every village also had respected medicine men and women, and specially appointed clan mothers and grandmothers.

Life went on nearly unchanged for hundreds of years for the Wampanoag. But by the 1700s, with the arrival of more and more Europeans, those who were still surviving were barely holding on to the customs and traditions of their ancestors.

A Wampanoag warrior in full battle dress

3 · WAMPANOAG BELIEFS

In the Wampanoag language there is no word for *religion*. But the Wampanoag have always had a deep spiritual connection to the world around them. They believe that everything comes from the Creator, or the Great Spirit, sometimes known as Kiehtan. They also believe that the Great Spirit made their bodies from the earth and the trees. In addition to the Great Spirit, the Wampanoag believe that a living spirit lies at the core of everything, from a river to a stone to a stalk of corn.

The Wampanoag see everything in the world as interconnected. Every part of their culture is valued as a gift from the Creator. To the early Wampanoag the land was the first and most precious gift. Corn was their most important crop, and a gift they could not live without. By living in harmony

The Wampanoag used this special stone, known as Indian Rock, to sharpen knives and other weapons and tools. The deep grooves in the rock are still clearly visible today.

The Giant, Moshup

Moshup is at the heart of many Wampanoag legends and beliefs. He was an ancient Wampanoag who, according to legend, took the form of a giant. Moshup created the islands off the coast of Massachusetts, including Noepe, or Martha's Vineyard. He was so huge, it was said, that he could step from one island to the next, as if they were stepping-stones.

An aerial view of Cape Cod, Massachusetts, and its surrounding islands—stepping-stones for the giant, Moshup.

Moshup taught the Wampanoag to fish and to hunt for whales. When he hunted whales himself he caught them with his bare hands. The Wampanoag believe that Moshup warned them of the coming of the settlers. He told them not to let the settlers onto their islands or they would be destroyed. But the Wampanoag were friendly people. When settlers came to Martha's Vineyard and Nantucket, the Wampanoag welcomed them. It did not take long for Moshup's prediction to come true.

According to Wampanoag tradition, Moshup waded away from the islands after warning his beloved people. He has not been seen since. When fog covers the islands, however, it is said to be the smoke from his pipe.

with the natural world—Mother Earth—the Wampanoag believed, they earned the many gifts their Creator provided.

The Wampanoag also believed in taking only what they needed from the land. To take more than this was wasteful, and being wasteful might anger the Creator. When an animal was killed for food the hunter prayed for forgiveness before taking its life. Ceremonies and feasts of thanksgiving are

Deer was an important part of the Wampanoag diet, but hunters never killed more than they needed.

At current-day powwows, Wampanoag men still perform the traditional bear dance dressed in real bearskins.

important rituals that, even now, take place many times during the year.

The Wampanoag language had no written form, so tribal history and other knowledge was passed down through stories. These stories, which often take the form of fairy tales and legends, have always been an important way for the

In the Wampanoag's traditional "Fire on the Water" ceremony, canoes carrying torches sail into the water. The ceremony's purpose is to celebrate the uniting of the four elements—earth, air, water, and fire.

Wampanoag people to share and protect their beliefs, traditions, and customs.

Even today these Wampanoag beliefs are held sacred. Modern-day Wampanoag feel strongly about protecting the land that has been given to them. They see their role as helping to preserve all of planet Earth, which they consider a gift from the Creator.

4 · A CHANGING WORLD

King Philip's War drastically reduced the Wampanoag population. Very few mainland Wampanoag managed to live through the battles. Most of the survivors later decided to **convert** to Christianity. The greatest number of survivors lived on Noepe, the island known today as Martha's Vineyard. Fewer Wampanoag were killed there because the island, being cut off from the fighting, was a fairly safe place. Another Massachusetts island, Nantucket, lost most of its Wampanoag when a wave of disease struck there in 1763.

After these tragedies the Wampanoag population gradually began to increase again. Today most Wampanoag live on the mainland around Cape Cod and on Martha's Vineyard, and they number about three thousand. Of these, most belong to

The cliffs of Gay Head, Massachusetts, where the Wampanoag fished, farmed, and hunted.

Modern-day Wampanoag have continued to keep their people's ancient rituals alive.

one of the five organized bands of Wampanoag, which include the Mashpee, the Assonet, the Herring Pond, the Namasket, and the Aquinnah, formerly called the Gay Head tribe. Other smaller bands also live in the region.

The Wampanoag have struggled for decades to gain federal recognition. As of early 2007, only the Mashpee and the Aquinnah had succeeded in this goal. Federal recognition has provided these tribes with government lands, money, and the right to govern themselves.

The Wampanoag have had many difficulties. But today they are fierce defenders of their nearly lost culture. They are American citizens, but they are doing everything they can to protect the knowledge that their ancestors passed down. They are relearning the ancient Wampanoag language and teaching their children native crafts and stories. Tribal members still serve in traditional roles, such as sachem and medicine man. In every way, the Wampanoag are dedicated to honoring the age-old traditions, ceremonies, and skills of their people.

Wampanoag Words

The Wampanoag spoke a language called Massachusett, one of many Algonquian languages. Tribes in southern New England spoke five different Algonquian languages, but these were close enough so that the tribes could understand each other. Here are some Wampanoag words.

Wampanoag Word	Pronounced	English Word
mishoon	mish-OON	dugout
weta	WAY-ta	woods
ohbee	OH-bee	earth
keegsquaw	KEEGS-kwa	maiden
ashaunt	ah-SHAWNT	lobster
natick	NAH-tic	place in the hills

Today, visitors to Massachusetts's Plimoth Plantation can explore an authentic Wampanoag village, built based on descriptions written in the 1600s. Here, a modern-day Wampanoag demonstrates the skill of making slates.

The ancestors of today's Wampanoag had one of the most important roles in U.S. history. Their descendents also have an important part to play. The modern "people of the early light" are the guardians of that history and of a rich culture that was almost lost.

· TIME LINE

Plymouth Colony is established on Wampanoag lands.

Wampanoag enter into peace treaty with Plymouth colonists.

Pilgrims celebrate first successful harvest with the Wampanoag.

Massasoit dies; Wamsutta becomes grand sachem.

Metacom, or "King Philip," becomes grand sachem.

Mounting conflict between English colonists and Wampanoag.

1620   1621   1621   1660   1662   1662–1675

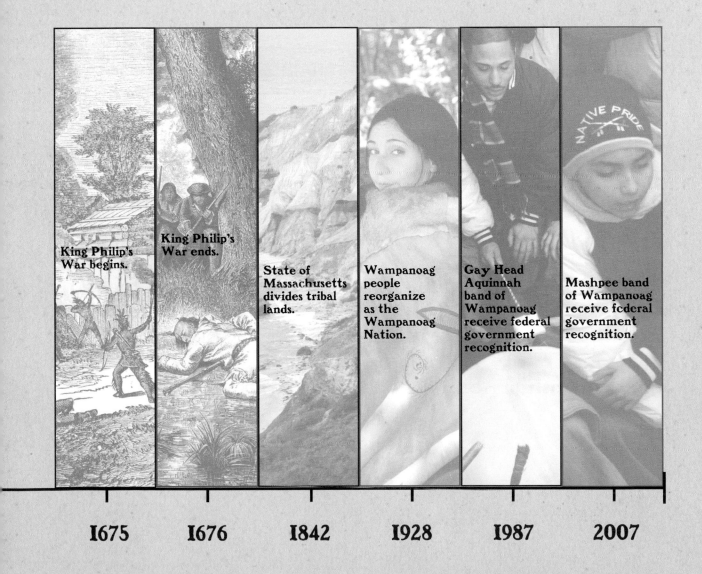

King Philip's War begins.

King Philip's War ends.

State of Massachusetts divides tribal lands.

Wampanoag people reorganize as the Wampanoag Nation.

Gay Head Aquinnah band of Wampanoag receive federal government recognition.

Mashpee band of Wampanoag receive federal government recognition.

1675 1676 1842 1928 1987 2007

· GLOSSARY

captives: People who have been caught and held against their will.

convert: To change one's religious beliefs from one system to another belief system.

dugouts: Canoes or boats made from a hollowed log.

lured: Attracted strongly.

mantle: A long cape that hangs over one shoulder.

marksmanship: Ability to shoot at a target, or mark.

moccasins: Shoes made from animal skin and stitched along the top edge.

pnieses: Powerful, highborn warriors who protected the sachem and did his or her bidding.

quahogs: Clams that have dark purple or white shells and are good to eat.

ravaged: Destroyed in a violent way.

sachem: Tribal chief.

wampum: Polished beads made from shells and strung together to be used as belts, ornaments, or money.

• FIND OUT MORE

Books

Bruchac, Joseph. *Squanto's Journey: The Story of the First Thanksgiving.* New York: Voyager Books/Harcourt, Inc., 2007.

Dell, Pamela. *Giles and Metacom: A Story of Plimoth Colony and the Wampanoag.* (Scrapbooks of America). Excelsior, MN: Tradition Books, 2003.

Gray-Kanatiiosh, Barbara A. *Wampanoag.* Edina, MN: Checkerboard Books, 2004.

Riehecky, Janet. *The Wampanoag: People of the First Light.* (American Indian Nations). New York: PowerKids Press/Rosen Publishing, 2005.

Web Sites

Plimoth Plantation
http://www.plimoth.org/kids/homeworkHelp/
This Web site will show you what life was like for both the Plymouth colonists and the Wampanoag.

The First Thanksgiving
http://www.history.com/minisites/thanksgiving/viewPage?pageId=872
All about the first Thanksgiving—including table manners.

About the Author

Pamela Dell is the author of over fifty books for children and young people. Her work includes nonfiction as well as both contemporary and historical fiction. She has written books about nature, history, and geography, as well as biographies. Pamela divides her time between Santa Monica, California, and Chicago.

· INDEX

Page numbers in **boldface** are illustrations.